The Internship
in Educational Administration

THE LIBRARY OF EDUCATION

A Project of The Center for Applied Research in Education, Inc.

G. R. Gottschalk, Director

Categories of Coverage

I	II	III
Curriculum and Teaching	Administration, Organization, and Finance	Psychology

IV	V	VI
History, Philosophy, and Social Foundations	Professional Skills	Educational Institutions

The Internship
in Educational Administration

DANIEL R. DAVIES

Professor of Education
Teachers College, Columbia University

1962
The Center for Applied Research in Education, Inc.
Washington, D. C.

Foreword

Because a profession cannot rise above the level of its individual members, programs which are designed to prepare individuals for a profession are of crucial importance. Experience seems to indicate clearly that the preparatory programs must be effective if a profession is to advance and improve.

Unlike some of the other professions, the profession of education has developed special programs for those who aspire to professional leadership positions. These programs, designed for the preparation of educational administrators, have a powerful impact upon the schools. They help in no small part to determine whether the administrators will promote creative teaching or deadly conformity, and strongly influence the level of leadership for the whole profession.

It is only within the last decade and a half that there has been any systematic attempt on a nation-wide scale to evaluate preparation programs for school administrators. Viewed in its historical perspective, this development may be taken as an indication of the vitality of the field. Programs of professional preparation for educational administrators did not begin to develop until the twentieth century, and it is nothing less than remarkable that within half a century of their inception these programs were already being searchingly evaluated.

Of the developments which have been an outgrowth of this evaluation, few—if any—will prove to be more significant, I believe, than the systematic use of internships. The fact that internships are proving themselves to be highly valuable in an administrator's preparation gives rise to the belief that the time may come when they will be considered indispensable.

The nation-wide evaluation effort, out of which internships have developed, has been promoted by the profession itself. The movement was initiated by the American Association of School Administrators, working cooperatively with other professional associations. It began with a meeting of professors of educational administration in Ithaca, New York, in the summer of 1947; continued with the organization of the National Conference of Professors of Educational Administration (NCPEA); expanded in the Cooperative Program in Educational Administration (CPEA), financed in considerable part by the W. K. Kellogg Foundation; and has achieved some degree of permanence in the University Council for Educational Administration (UCEA), an organization dedicated to the upgrading of educational administration and composed of leading universities throughout the country.

Dr. Daniel R. Davies has been closely involved in all these developments. Born in Pennsylvania in 1911, he had experience both as a teacher and as an administrator before joining the staff at Teachers College, Columbia University, where he is now Professor of Education. He has written numerous books and articles and has had a number of distinguished editorial and consulting assignments. A leader in the early meetings of professors of educational administration, he was the Coordinator of the CPEA in the Middle Atlantic Region from 1950 to 1959 and was the first executive director of the UCEA. He has been in a strategic position to view many research projects and experiments in administration, including a variety of internship programs. He is thus peculiarly well fitted for writing the present volume.

This volume constitutes an excellent synopsis of the literature in this area. As such, it should prove useful to all those who want an overview of the field. It contains many ideas which should prove helpful in the initiation or operation of internship programs, and thus should be of special interest to administrators, school board members, teachers, and citizens. Teacher educators who have responsibilities for internship programs should also find this volume useful.

CLARENCE A. NEWELL
*Professor of Educational
Administration*
University of Maryland

Contents

CHAPTER V

Effects of Internship Programs   84

CHAPTER VI

Summary and Predictions   95

Bibliography   100

Appendix   107

Index   115

The Internship
in Educational Administration

CHAPTER I

Presenting the Internship

The internship in educational administration is a part of the recommended program of preparation for persons aspiring to become administrators of schools, school systems, and colleges. The internship focuses upon training, development and educational experiences for those persons in actual school situations.

The term "internship" is borrowed directly from the medical profession. Medical educators apply the word to the hospital experience required of every medical doctor near or at the end of his college preparation program before he can be licensed to practice medicine. He must, in other words, have "field" experience under the guidance of veteran practitioners before he is allowed to practice on his own. The internship is an integral part of his professional preparation.

Until comparatively recently the administrative internship in education has not been clearly and carefully defined. Experimental internship programs have taken many forms. To the extent that these differences represent useful experimentation, they have been helpful. But many of the programs which a few years ago were referred to as "internships" actually were not such at all, as the term is now defined. It is important, therefore, to keep clearly in mind what the internship *is* and what it *is not*.

What the internship is. In order to constitute a bona fide internship in educational administration, the following conditions must be satisfied:

1. The student's field experience which is labeled "internship" is an integral part of his professional education which comes after or near the completion of his formal program of professional preparation.
2. His internship involves a considerable block of time—at least one semester on a full-time basis or the equivalent.
3. The student must be expected to carry real and continuous responsibilities in his field situation under the competent supervision of a practicing administrator.

4. The board of education or board of trustees of the institution in which he is interning supports the program at the policy level.

5. The professional school in which he is enrolled is joint sponsor of his program along with the school system or institution. The professional school also assists in his supervision.

Two additional conditions are highly desirable:

1. The state department of education recognizes and endorses the internship program for the state as a whole.

2. The national and state associations of educational administrators are on record as endorsing—and even requiring—the internship as part of each practitioner's preparation and as part of his requirement for membership in the respective associations.

Thus, an internship in educational administration is a phase of professional preparation in which a student who is nearing the completion of his formal study works in the field under the competent supervision of a practicing administrator and of a professional school representative for a considerable block of time for the purpose of developing competence in carrying administrative responsibilities.[1] The program, in addition, is soundly based upon the state's legal structure through the state education department and upon the approved standards of the profession through its associations.

What the internship is not. The internship is *not* an apprenticeship. There are a number of similarities which make it easy to confuse the two. Both involve direct, on-the-job experience. The difference is largely one of timing and degree of difficulty. Unfortunately, the two terms tend to be used interchangeably in practice. It is important, therefore, to clarify their differences.[2]

Apprenticeship is the term applied to an on-the-job experience program, usually in the candidate's own school system or institution. There may or may not be a working relationship with a professional school to assist in the process. The initiative lies with the

---

[1] Clarence A. Newell, *Handbook for the Development of Internship Programs in Educational Administration* (New York: Cooperative Program in Educational Administration, Middle Atlantic Region, Teachers College, Columbia University, May 1952), p. 4.

[2] Newell, "Internships and Apprenticeships in Educational Administration," *American School Board Journal,* 129 (July 1954), p. 26.

school or institution, which selects promising candidates, gives them direct practice under the supervision of its own administrators, and even helps each candidate decide whether or not he should seek formal training required for the license.

At its best, the apprenticeship is part of a total "executive development" program. For example, in a northern New York school system both the apprenticeship and the internship are employed. The apprenticeship is intended to offer *career guidance* to the teachers of the school system and to stimulate the continuing supply of able replacements for administrative vacancies. Each year three apprenticeships are offered. Teachers who are interested in exploring the area of administration are urged to apply. They need have had no formal training in administration, although their having had a limited amount will not exclude them.

Because far more apply than can be accommodated in any one year, a screening committee reviews the applications and credentials of each applicant. Three are chosen. Those who are unsuccessful may reapply annually as often as they wish. The chosen three are relieved of their regular assignments for the year and are replaced with a rotating trio of permanent teachers who are employed for this purpose.

For the whole year, then, each of the apprentices works closely with and observes a principal or someone on the central administrative staff. Each may have a wide and rich variety of assignments. But here the second chief difference between the apprenticeship and the internship is evident. The apprentice's assignments are more elementary and are largely exploratory. At the end of the year each expects to return to his teaching post.

What are the consequences? Several. The teacher may decide that the administrative life is not for him. In that case, the incident is closed. If, however, he decides that his future lies in administration, a further evaluation is made by those who have been observing him. They may believe him unsuited for administration and may advise him to seek his further career in education in the classroom or in some other nonadministrative position. On the other hand, they may strongly encourage him to begin formal training in educational administration at once. But in no case does the school system specifically promise a principalship or other administrative post to the apprentice.

Notice that the emphasis in this example of the apprenticeship is on career guidance. The apprenticeship year is an exploratory one, both for the teacher and for the school system. One interesting outcome of the plan is that far more potential administrators are discovered than could ever possibly be employed within the system. And the supply continues. Why? Because the school board and administration freely and generously recommend able apprentices who acquire the needed extra formal training for administrative positions in other school systems.

Do not, then, confuse the internship with the apprenticeship. The internship emphasizes rigorous learning experiences in the field near the end of a formal preparation program. It assumes that the candidate's basic decision to become an administrator has long since been made. The apprenticeship emphasizes career guidance and exploration. Formal training in administration may not yet have begun. If it has, it is still in the introductory stage. The apprentice's role is primarily observational. His operational duties are likely to be nonsensitive and elementary. Routine but necessary duties of the administrator figure prominently in his assignments.

As a further description of the apprenticeship, let us look at how it operates in a school system in California:[3]

> To become an administrative training candidate at Campbell, one must have completed two years of satisfactory teaching experience, finished his military obligation, been accepted for graduate level work at college, completed six units of upper division work, and been awarded a California teaching credential.
>
> The candidate then makes a formal application to the selection committee of district administrators and is given a series of tests by Stanford University. The selection committee interviews each candidate, observes his classroom teaching, evaluates him with his building principal, and rates the candidate on the basis of what they have learned about him. After all the candidates have been screened, the committee then selects five for the program.
>
> Each trainee is assigned a principal for an advisor. The advisor helps him plan his program of visitations, informs the trainee of

[3] Fred Peterson, "An Administrative Trainee Looks at the Program," *Administrative Training Bulletin* (Santa Clara County, San Jose, California, 1958).

helpful experience available as the semester progresses, and evaluates the work of the trainee.

The trainee is given one day of released time every two weeks during the first semester of the program. This time is spent visiting each school in the district, the superintendent, the assistant superintendent, and the business manager for a half-day each.

Through these visits, the trainee becomes better acquainted with the administrators, the schools, the teachers, and the general policies of the district. While the first semester is mainly a "familiarization" period, the second semester is more flexible, and the trainee can schedule work which will suit his particular needs and interests.

In the second semester, most trainees try to spend the bulk of their time in actual teaching and curriculum work in areas with which they are least familiar. In 1958, for the first time, trainees have been accepted for a third semester and are working with the district curriculum coordinator in improving and evaluating the courses of instruction.

The trainees actually participate in many other phases of the total district program, especially in areas in which they feel the greatest need. To name all the activities would be difficult, but some of the more common functions are attending all board meetings; attending principals' meetings, working with PTA and other community groups, classroom teaching on all levels; assisting their own principal in pupil accounting, budget preparation, student counseling duty, and class schedule preparation, substitute and student teacher orientation, teacher evaluation, etc.; inter-district visitation; house counts; and participating in and leading educational discussion groups and workshops.

Clearly, then, the internship is not an apprenticeship; nor is it to be thought of as a kind of cheap labor. There have been cases where a so-called internship was nothing more than a ruse for hiring an advanced graduate student to do a needed chore in the central office.

Suppose, for example, that the school board wants a study made of the success of its high school graduates in college. The superintendent reviews the assignments of the various members of his staff and concludes that there is none available who can assume the extra burden. A good solution would be a part-time, temporary appointment of a person who knew the field of education well.

Such a job would be just the spot for a graduate student—an intern. One is found from among the ranks of full-time students in a neighboring university, and the unfortunate victim spends his days doing one task with little opportunity to view the whole perspective of the administrative job. The school system profits from the services of an eager, capable young professional who is in direct contact with some of the most recent ideas and developments in education, who is a nontenure appointment, and who can be paid a nominal salary.

Such "internships" are not internship programs at all. Applying the term thusly can bring disfavor and discredit to the whole internship idea. Fortunately, distortions and prostitutions of this sort are becoming fewer and fewer as agreement spreads concerning the operational meaning of the term "internship."

Internship versus Externship

Another source of confusion exists. Strictly speaking, the discussion of the "externship," has been thus far as the term is often used in the medical profession. The distinction is based upon the place of residence of the student. If he lives *in the hospital* during the period of his field experience, he is an *intern*. If he lives elsewhere—for example, at the university—and commutes daily to the hospital, he is an *extern*.

To apply the same distinction to the field of education would require our calling "interns" those who actually move to and reside in the community where they are practicing. Conversely, those students who choose to live at the university and to travel daily to the school system would be "externs."

Since practically none of the cases of what are called internships in educational administration call for the student's actually living on the school grounds (possible exceptions: interns in the college deanship, where the student might be expected to live on the campus), the term "externship" might have been a better one. The distinction, however, is not made in the field of education. Both are included under the one term: internship.

The field of hospital administration solved the matter of terminology neatly. Currently, to acquire a master's degree in hospital administration, a student typically spends one full "didactic" year in classes on the university campus. Then he spends a "residency" year—what we would call a year's internship—in a hospital, which generally is many miles from the campus of the university.

The Internship in Perspective

The internship and the externship is more than a matter of terminology. The fundamental question is the relationship of laboratory and field experience to the verbal classroom experience of the learner. Few would disagree that classroom lessons can be scaled in difficulty from introductory and simple to advanced and complex. Indeed, every teacher attempts so to arrange his lessons, his teaching, and his syllabus. Field and laboratory experiences can also be scaled in difficulty. On such a scale, observation is at one end and responsibility for decision and action at the other.

In a continuum of field experiences from elementary to advanced, internship as here presented belongs at the extreme end of advancement. It is the final stage before the student is awarded an advanced degree or certificate from the professional school, before he is awarded a license by the state to administer, before he is granted full membership in his professional society, and before he is hired for the first time as an administrator.

At the beginning of the scale would be apprenticeships and field trips from the university for the purpose of observing. Next in order of difficulty come such activities as special field projects and participation in surveys, always under the supervision and direction of a professor from the university. Toward the advanced end of this phase of field experiences comes the typical doctoral project or dissertation, to the extent that it is oriented toward direct field activity and research. In practice to date, the doctoral project usually comes after the internship because a license to practice in educational administration is nowhere yet contingent upon the possession of the doctorate. Hence, doctoral study is more like *in-service* education for the administrator who will have been practicing for some time. The trend of the times, however, is toward more and more preparation prior to licensure.

Overlappings and even reversals of the above described sequences currently occur in practice. The confusion lies in the loose use of terms, in disagreements as to best practice, and in a healthy ferment of theory and concept about the very positions for which internship is thought to prepare students. The preponderance of informed opinion and of best practice, however, supports the definition of the internship here presented, and its place in the hierarchy of field experiences.

Where Internships Have Occurred

Applications of the internship have touched almost all possible kinds of administrative positions both in and related to education. The "school type" internship has been taken with the elementary principal, the junior high school principal, the senior high school principal, the assistant superintendent for instruction, the assistant superintendent for business, and with the superintendent himself. By far the most common type has been the internship with the superintendent.

Interns have served with county superintendents of schools, and in state education departments. In the latter agency the possibilities are rich. Interns have been placed successfully with state commissioners of education and with assistant commissioners for research, for finance, for curriculum, and the like. The trainees' career possibilities are greatly enhanced by this state-wide view of education that they receive—an opportunity that otherwise might never come to them. Some have chosen to stay in state department work; others have gone out from such internships into local superintendencies, into college professorships, and into positions in national agencies.

Interns have served in state and national education agencies and associations. The need for specific preparation for administrative positions in state and national education associations has led to experimentation with the internship at those levels. One intern with the National Education Association was given the opportunity to assist with the conducting of regional meetings in a number of spots over the United States. The view of education at work nationally that he received could scarcely be duplicated otherwise. Planning for this kind of internship emphasizes a variety of administrative and supervisory experiences, including those that take place in the central office in connection with research studies as well as in field services.

Interns have served with publishing companies which cater to the field of educational administration. Teachers College, Columbia University, and New York University have sponsored administrative internships with the American School Publishing Company. In this case the interns worked as "directors of research" under the direct supervision of the editor-in-chief. They had unusual opportunities to travel widely to conventions and professional meetings, to meet the leaders of the profession, to look for publishable material, to edit and to write, to conduct administrative research, and to acquire practice in conference leadership. Some question whether this type of experience is really internship for field administrative positions such as the superintendency. It is, indeed, a good question. No one quarrels with the great value to the intern in professional stimulation and extension of his horizons. But is it, strictly speaking, an internship unless the student elects to stay in an administrative role in magazine publishing?

Interns have served in the administrative offices of colleges and universities. The possibilities here are wide, too. Interns have been placed with administrative deans, presidents, registrars, admissions officers, vice-presidents in charge of development, superintendents of buildings and grounds, and bursars. The results have been excellent in most cases. Young men and young women who have interned in such positions almost without fail have been placed in comparable positions advantageously.

Interns have served with school architects. The population explosion puts school building planning, financing, construction, and remodeling in the center of administrative problems. Architectural firms by the hundreds have entered the school building field. They find that they need persons with a background both in educational administration and in education widely who can talk intelligently with school officials as potential clients. The internship in this case prepares students for "account executive" type positions with architectural firms.

Interns have served with consultant firms of several kinds. The number and variety of such firms increase annually. Some specialize in advising boards and administrators at both the lower school level and at the college level on their building needs. In effect, they act as go-betweens in the board-architect relations. Other firms offer more general service, including advice in personnel administration, organization, business procedures—in fact, the whole gamut of administrative matters.

Except for the "school type" positions listed above, the others are often referred to as "fringe type" positions. Until recently, specific preparation for them was not offered. By way of the internship, existing patterns of formal preparation are readily adaptable to their specific requirements. In this sense, the internship is an adaptability factor in professional school programs for preparing educational administrators.

Purposes and Values of Internship

The internship in educational administration, like any other program of instruction, is intended to satisfy certain objectives. Unfortunately, complete statements or lists of such objectives have not been compiled. A thorough study of the available articles and books on the topic produced the following composite list of objectives.[4] They fall into three categories: those applicable to the intern, to the sponsoring field agency, and to the cooperating university.

Objectives applicable to the intern.

To enable the intern to develop a more comprehensive view of educational administration.

> The difference between what is taught in the professional schools and what actually occurs in the day-to-day, practicing situation sometimes is substantial. The reasons are many: The lag between theory and practice; gaps in the professional curriculum; nuances of operations dealing with real people that are difficult to tell about in the lecture hall; effects of community pressures for specific changes. These and other extensions of the on-campus part of his professional preparation come to him, it is said, by way of the internship.

To provide the intern with the experience of carrying real administrative responsibility.

> The purpose here is to offer direct experience as a teacher,

---

[4] Cooperative Program in Educational Administration, Middle Atlantic Region, *Appraisal of the Internship in Educational Administration*, Clifford P. Hooker, ed. (New York: Teachers College, Columbia University, 1958), p. 5.

rather than relying on the vicarious experience of the campus classroom. Much of administration involves *action skills*. To learn skills,
study them, try them, practice them, eliminate incorrect ones, and
thus perfect correct ones. The intern learns how to perfect his
skills under the pressure of responsibility.

To enable the intern to benefit from lessons learned by the sponsoring administrator during long professional experience.

Here is an ideal "Mark Hopkins on one end of a log, and I on
the other" situation. It is a teacher-pupil ratio of 1:1. The sponsoring administrator has what Alfred North Whitehead once referred
to as power based upon the reality of direct experience, and in the
tutorial relationship he can use it to the maximum to the benefit
of the intern.

To provide a testing ground for the beginning educator whereby the
adequacy of his training, probable success as an administrator, and the
type of position for which he is best suited can be determined.

Just as automobile manufacturers need "proving grounds" and
road tests to check the dependability and performance of their
laboratory-designed and factory-built products, so do professional
schools need a safety check on their selection and developmental
processes. Here is the guidance function of the internship. Like
the automobile road tests, it assumes the basic soundness of the
product. It is pointed primarily at correcting details of design and
manufacture—and estimating the probable market.

To instill in the intern a correct interpretation of the code of professional ethics.

As is the case with the Golden Rule and the Ten Command-
ments, it is one thing to know them by heart and to know what
they mean to the extent that round-table discussions can interpret
them. It is quite another problem to know how and when to apply
them in practice. The utility of a code of ethics to a profession and
to the public depends upon the extent to which the practitioners
individually know how to apply the code, and do so.

Objectives applicable to the sponsoring administrator.

To provide opportunity for administrators and field agencies to fulfill
their obligation of sharing in the preparation of prospective administrators.

The assumption here is that the continuity and development of a
profession is a wide-spread responsibility, especially in the public
service of education. Continuity and development of capable administrative leadership, then, is not the sole responsibility of the
professional school, and should never be so conceived. Practicing
administrators, school systems, county and state education offices,

professional associations and agencies at local, state, and national levels—all can best be thought of as extensions of the professional school's campus in this sense.

To provide the sponsoring administrator with professional counsel from the staff of the cooperating university.

The intern becomes a "communication bridge" between his sponsoring administrator and the latest ideas, theory, research, and experimentation being discussed and taught on the campus. In addition, supervisory visits by the professor-representative to the sponsoring administrator and to the intern provide another such "bridge" between "town and gown."

To provide additional services for the sponsoring field agency.

By relating problems of the field agency to his regular class work, the intern can offer an analysis and possible solutions to those problems under the guidance of his professors. Term papers, field projects and controlled experimentation can be done to the advantage of the field agency—and usually at no extra cost to the agency.

To stimulate the professional growth of the sponsoring administrator.

One of the best ways to learn is to teach. Each sponsoring administrator has the task of coaching a bright young student who is in touch with the latest and best that the professional school has to offer. Old, out-moded ideas and practices of the sponsoring administrator may not stand up very well—either in his own eyes or in the eyes of the intern. In his zeal to justify being continued as a sponsoring administrator, he must necessarily read, study, and travel to keep abreast of latest developments in the profession. Teaching the inexperienced is a challenge to the experienced.

To provide a means for evaluating administrative ability in prospective administrators.

A succession of interns gives the sponsoring administrator a chance to look over possible permanent employees without feeling any commitment to any one of the interns individually. In this sense, the internship becomes an extension of the recruitment and selection process of the field agency for maintaining its own supply of administrators.

Objectives applicable to the cooperating university.

To test the training program of the professional school against reality in the field and thereby to improve that program's effectiveness for preparing prospective administrators.

Feed-back from both the intern and the sponsoring administrator gives important clues to the professional school concerning strengths and weaknesses of its curriculum and teaching. Just as automobile manufacturers correct design and manufacturing processes in the

light of road testing and consumer use-experience, so can professional school faculties check and correct their operations.

To stimulate the interaction of the university and the surrounding
school districts and other educational agencies.

Research and experience in several professional fields—education
and medicine, for example—show that when there are many con-
tacts between the professional school and the field agencies and
practitioner, the quality of performance of both improves. Con-
tacts which begin with the internship frequently lead to others
equally rewarding.

To encourage the in-service development of professors of educational
administration.

Professors who have direct contact with field problems are much
less liable to the charge that they live in an ivory tower. In the
process of supervising internships, they have their theories, ideas
and recommended practices tested regularly and rigorously against
the hard facts of daily school operation. They can adjust what they
teach, and bring in new, up-to-date illustrations to use in their
classroom teaching. Having observed *what is* personally, they are
in a much better position to expound on *what should be*.

Professor Internships
in Educational Administration

One other type of internship should be presented. Strictly speaking, it is not an internship in administration; it is an internship in
the teaching of administration. Because it is directly related to education, administration, and internship, and because it is a direct
outgrowth of the internship movement in educational administration, it belongs in this discussion—even though peripherally.

The professor internship began in 1951 through the efforts of the
Cooperative Program in Educational Administration, Middle Atlantic Region.[5] As of that time a few colleges had internship programs of the kind previously discussed, but the professor internship
was a departure from the practice current at that time. During the
ensuing few years, nearly a dozen persons intending to become professors in this area of specialization served internships.

The professor internship in educational administration under-
takes to identify and to select capable persons for positions as pro-

---

[5] B. J. Chandler and D. R. Davies, "Professor Internships in Educational Administration," *Teachers College Record*, Vol. 54, No. 4 (January 1953), pp. 202–
208.

fessors of educational administration, to develop teaching and other professorial competencies in those selected, and to provide on-the-job training.

To some extent the professor internship rests upon the same principle as the graduate assistantship. However, *it is far more comprehensive.* The CPEA stipulated that the intern should be given opportunity to experience all of the significant activities of a regular college teacher of educational administration. He should not be expected to spend much time on trivial or purely clinical duties, nor should he be considered as a "graduate assistant," "reader," or "clerk."

Several purposes for the professor internship were defined:

1. To provide a period of practical experience to supplement the intern's previous preparation by working as a member of a college instructional staff under the guidance of professors of recognized proficiency.
2. To provide competent professional assistance to college departments of Educational Administration in the development of improved programs for the preparation of educational leaders.
3. To provide a supply of well-qualified men to fill future college positions as professors of educational administration.

Impetus for experimentation with the professor internship came from a follow-up study of doctoral graduates (of Teachers College, Columbia University, between 1935 and 1945) whose major field was the general administration of school systems. About 50 per cent of those graduates went into professorships in educational administration rather than into the superintendencies for which they were prepared, and yet no attempt was being made to differentiate between preparation programs for the professorship and those for the superintendency. The question arose as to whether a typical doctoral program designed to prepare field administrators was also necessarily the best to equip professors to teach administration to others.

Experience with the professor internship, brief as it has been, shows clearly that the tasks, knowledge, and skills required of the professorship are not the same as those required for the superintendency.

Unfortunately, the idea of the professor internship has not caught on in the profession. It is not known whether any examples now exist. It may be that the whole tradition of denial of the need for specific instruction and supervised practice in the arts of teaching at the collegiate level dies hard. At any rate, a major task that confronts professional schools preparing potential professors of educational administration is to devise effective patterns of organization and programs of instruction that will provide realistic training for the prospective professor—and that means internship experience, too.

Summary

The internship in educational administration is a learning experience for the trainee. It comes near the end of his formal, preparatory program. It is not to be confused with other kinds of valuable field experience, such as the apprenticeship.

The internship's values and purposes go beyond those for the intern, himself. There are some as well for the sponsoring administrator, for the field agency, and for the cooperating university. It has even been suggested that professors who aspire to teach educational administration should themselves serve internships.

CHAPTER II

Origins and Development
of the Internship

Internships for prospective school administrators are almost wholly a development of the second half of the twentieth century. Before 1947 only two universities claim to have done any experimenting with the idea.

The introduction and development of the internship idea in educational administration followed and paralleled similar developments in other fields, chiefly medicine. Medical students who had studied in Europe in the latter part of the Nineteenth Century imported the internship pattern into the United States. Why the term "intern" was adopted rather than "extern" is not known. The former referred to a student who boarded at the school where he studied. The latter referred to a student who studied at a school but did not board there. Over the years "internship" came to be applied to both patterns in this country, signifying a period of professional education in which the student would try out his classroom-learned knowledge and skills in actual field situations under competent supervision.

Internships became firmly established as a necessary part of the development of physicians. Gradually internships appeared in other professions such as public administration, library science, the ministry, nursing, social welfare, and teaching. In the field of education, student teaching has become well-established as a part of the professional preparation of teachers. Internships for professors of educational administration appeared in the 1950's with the financial support of the W. K. Kellogg Foundation.

Two events in the field of educational administration gave substantial impetus to the spread of the internship approach. The first was the organization of the National Conference of Professors of Educational Administration under the leadership of Walter Cocking. Prior to the first annual meeting of that organization in the summer of 1947 at Endicott, New York, few professors of educational administration knew many others on a personal basis. Nationally known names—previously known to most of the members merely as names on books, articles and research papers—at last became associated with real people. The step to first-name relations was easy in the informal, intimate living arrangements of a camp ground. The possibilities of easy, quick communication among the leaders in the professorship of educational administration increased enormously.

One topic of general interest was the internship. Two universities, the University of Chicago and the University of Omaha, reported experience with the program—the former since 1933 and the latter since 1946. Others had been tentatively exploring the idea. It soon became apparent that many of the men present wanted ample opportunity to discuss the nature of the internship, its pros and cons, and the ways to organize a new internship program on a university campus.

As a result, "interest groups" were set up which continued through several summer meetings. General sessions of the total membership heard reports of the interest groups and discussed them heatedly. Some professors thought that internships in school administration were neither feasible nor desirable. Others believed that they were a must. In between, those professors who had tried the internship approach described what they had done and what they proposed to do.

The academic year 1947–48, following the first summer's conference, began to show results of the discussions. Five universities inaugurated internship programs. They varied widely in their design. Some provided that an intern should carry extensive administrative responsibilities; others provided only for observation. Some provided for supervision of the intern by a sponsoring administrator and by a university representative; others provided for no supervision. Some insisted that the intern be paid for his services; others required no salary. Some listed the internship in the university catalogue with definite numbers of credits assigned to the experience; others did not.

The actual situation in 1949–50 is shown in the Wheaton status study of internships in educational administration which appeared that year[1] Wheaton explored the experiences of universities, students, and sponsoring agencies in internship programs. Of 152 professional schools surveyed, he found that:

1. Seventeen were operating internship programs.
2. Seven were operating modified programs.
3. Five were actively considering the idea of organizing in the near future.
4. Eleven stated that they were interested generally but were taking no active steps.
5. None of the others reported any interest.

Details of the history and development of internships in the seventeen professional schools which reported operating programs are given in Table 1. Several conclusions are directly apparent from the data. First, the number of students serving internships in relation to the total number of majors in educational administration per institution is low. If the internship were to become a part of *each* student's experience, the problem of numbers would have to be faced. Second, no standards had been reached as to credit allocation for the program. Third, no agreement existed as to the graduate level at which the internship should be offered.

The second of the two major developments that contributed to the rapid extension of the internship idea in educational administration was the appearance of the Cooperative Program in Educational Administration (CPEA) in 1950, financed by a grant of several millions of dollars from the W. K. Kellogg Foundation. The nation-wide program was administered through eight university centers. Each was committed to work on the development of improved programs for selecting and preparing school administrators, and for the continued in-service growth of men already on the job. Each center worked out a plan independently of the others but within the over-all objectives of the CPEA.

The center at Teachers College, Columbia University, chose as one of its special purposes to encourage experimentation with and

---

[1] Gordon A. Wheaton, *A Status Study of Internship Programs in School Administration,* A Report of a Type C Project (New York: Teachers College, Columbia University, 1950).

extension of the internship approach to preparing school administrators. Other centers, without concentrating on the problem, also
made contributions, notably Harvard under the direction of Professors Cyril Sargent and Alfred Simpson, and Ohio State University under the direction of Professor John Ramseyer.

In the first year of the CPEA at Teachers College, John H.
Fischer, on leave from his position as Assistant Superintendent of
Schools in Baltimore, Maryland, coordinated the internship phase
of the project, relieving Professor Daniel R. Davies, who had begun
the internship program at the college in 1947. By the spring of
1951 enough had been accomplished to warrant holding the first
Middle Atlantic States Work Conference on Internships in Educational Administration. Representatives of more than a dozen universities from North Carolina through New York State participated.

The results of the conference were so favorable that members of
the group requested a progress report to help them solve internship
problems on their home campuses. Consequently, the executive
committee of the CPEA-MAR agreed in January of 1952 to seek
the help of Professor Clarence A. Newell of the University of
Maryland. They asked him to assemble materials from the conference and from any other available sources and to prepare a manual
on how to establish and conduct internship programs in educational
administration. This he agreed to do, and the manual was published
in May, 1952.[2]

In November, 1952, ten men joined in discussing "Internships in
School Administration" in a lengthy portfolio in *The Nation's
Schools*. Who they were and why they were asked to participate is
significant in the history of evolution of the internship in educational
administration in the United States. They are to be numbered
among the pioneers in the field:

1. Clarence A. Newell, Professor of Educational Administration, University of Maryland.
2. William A. Yeager, Professor of Educational Administration, University of Pittsburgh.

---

[2] Clarence A. Newell, *Handbook for the Development of Internship Programs
in Educational Administration* (New York: Cooperative Program in Educational
Administration, Middle Atlantic Region, Teachers College, Columbia University,
May 1952), 55 pp.

TABLE 1

INTERNSHIP PROGRAMS FOR SCHOOL ADMINISTRATORS—
HISTORY AND DEVELOPMENT BY 17 TRAINING INSTITUTIONS

Training Institution	1	2	3	4	5	6	7	8	9	10
Colorado: Colorado State College of Education	Winter 1949–1950	2 3 1	Superintendency (local) Secondary principalships Unclassified	6	Yes	Yes	8 per quarter semester	Master's 8 Doctorate 16	16%	Either level, providing course requirements are met
Florida: John B. Stetson University	Spring 1949–1950	2	Secondary Principalships	4	Yes	Yes	10 credit hours per semester	—	—	—
Georgia: University of Georgia	1947	4 8 1	Secondary Principalships Elementary Principalships Junior High Principalship	33	Yes	Yes	5 quarter hours may be earned per nine month school term	Masters	10%	Masters level
Illinois: University of Chicago	Prior to 1940	1	Secondary Principalship Elementary Principalship	150	Yes	Yes	No limit for resident students	—	—	—
Southern Illinois University	Winter 1949–1950	2 1 2	Secondary Principalship Elementary Principalships Supervisors	5	Yes	Yes	16 per year	Masters 16	—	Masters level

Institution	Date		Positions				Requirements	Degree	%	Level/Notes
Indiana: Ball State Teachers College	Summer 1949	1 1 5 3	Superintendency (county) Superintendency (local) Secondary Principalships Elementary Principalships	10	Yes	Yes	5 term hours per semester for principal internships 8 term hours per semester for superintendency internships	Doctorate 16	—	Either level, providing course requirements are met
Maryland: University of Maryland	Spring 1947–1948	2	Supervisors	9	Yes	Yes	12 to 16 per semester	Any degree 16	—	Depends upon student and school situation
Western Maryland College	Winter 1948	1 1	Asst. Superintendency (county) Secondary Principalship	5	Yes	Yes	15 per semester	Masters 15	50%	Masters level
Massachusetts: Harvard University	New plan 1950	2	—	2	No	No	—	—	—	Advanced study on doctoral level Arrangements on individual basis
Michigan: Michigan State College	Winter 1948	—	State Dept. of Public Instruction	2	No	No	None	None	—	Doctoral level
Nebraska: University of Omaha	Winter 1946	2	Secondary Principalships	4	No	Yes	3 credit hours per semester	Masters 3	10%	Masters level

TABLE 1 (Cont.)

Institution	Date	Positions	No.			Credit requirement	Degree	Percent	Doctoral level
New York: Teachers College, Columbia University	Winter 1947–1948	Superintendency (local) 3, Secondary Principalship 1, Elementary Principalship 3	26	Yes	Yes	4 credit hours per semester	Doctoral 8	9%	Doctoral level
Cornell University	Winter 1948–1949	— 0	4	Yes	Yes	6 credit hours per semester	Masters 6 Doctors 6	20% M.A. 6% Doct.	Either level depending upon circumstances
New York University	1949–1950	Secondary Principalship 2, Elementary Principalship 1, Supervisors 2, State Dept. Officials 2	7	Yes	Yes	6 credit hours per semester	Masters or Doctorate 12	20% M.A. 25% Doct.	Either level providing foundational course requirements are met
Syracuse University	Winter 1949–1950	Secondary Principalship 1	1	Yes	Yes	3 credit hours per semester	Masters or Doctorate	—	Either level providing other requirements are met
University of Buffalo	Winter 1949–1950	Secondary Principalship 1	1	No	Yes	—	—	—	Either level. Teaching exper. Required